By the Lake

Dona Herweck Rice

Publishing Credits

Rachelle Cracchiolo, M.S.Ed., *Publisher*
Conni Medina, M.A.Ed., *Managing Editor*
Nika Fabienke, Ed.D., *Content Director*
Véronique Bos, *Creative Director*
Shaun N. Bernadou, *Art Director*
Valerie Morales, *Associate Editor*
John Leach, *Assistant Editor*
Courtney Roberson, *Senior Graphic Designer*

Image Credits: All images from iStock and/or Shutterstock.

Teacher Created Materials
5301 Oceanus Drive
Huntington Beach, CA 92649-1030
www.tcmpub.com
ISBN 978-1-4938-9840-4
© 2019 Teacher Created Materials, Inc.
Printed in China
Nordica.082018.CA21800936

Go and find some

 by the water.

flowers

Go and find some

 by the water.

trees

Go and find some

 by the water.

sticks

Go and find some 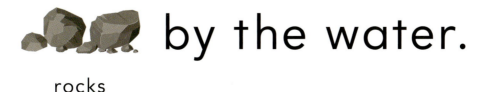 by the water.

rocks

Go and find some  by the water.

mud

Go and find some  by the water.

sand

Go and find some

turtles
by the water.

Go and find some 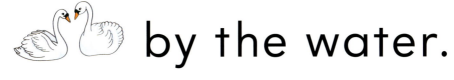 by the water.

swans

Go and find some  by the water.

boats

Go and find some  by the water.

kids

High-Frequency Words

New Words

by   find

go   some

water

Review Words

and   the